M000073021

my own mind, there is no coincidence between the awakening c
men and the fall of the Berlin Wall, the end of the Cold War; peac
Ireland; and the development of minority rights in our culture. In th
cent of women is a powerful engine for positive change within socie
For the Love of Women is about the real power of women. Th
ver manifests itself in so many ways that we can hardly realize th
act upon our daily lives. In the mid-sixties, when women realize

and be admired. Women want to get married and have kids
men want to make men happy just as before. But not be effaced
e doing it. Women want to be women but also demand respect and
loyalty from their men. For the Love of Women is a series of
amic snapshots of women. Women who love and want to be love

n my own mind, there is no coincidence between the awakening of w
nd the fall of the Berlin Wall, the end of the Cold War; pea
reland; and the development of minority rights in our culture.
scent of women is a powerful engine for positive change within s

respect and true loyalty from their men. For the Love of Wome
series of dynamic snapshots of women. Women who love and wan
ove. Women who work hard and want the rewards that are co

For the Love of
Women

This book belongs to

© 2000 Modus Vivendi Publishing Inc.
All rights reserved.

Published by:
Modus Vivendi Publishing Inc.
3859 Laurentian Autoroute
Laval, Quebec
Canada H7L 3H7
or
2565 Broadway, Suite 161
New York, New York 10025

Cover: Marc Alain

Picture Credits: © 1997 Wood River Gallery and SuperStock

Legal Deposit: 3rd Quarter, 2000
National Library of Canada

Canadian Cataloguing in Publication Data
Anderson, Marie
    For the Love of Women
    (Heartfelt Series)
    ISBN: 2-89523-024-2
    1. Women. 2. Women – Pictorial works. I. Title.
    II. Series
HQ1233.D4713 2000   305.4   C00941187-9

Canada We acknowledge the financial support of the Government
of Canada through the Book Publishing Industry Development
Program (BPIDP) for our publishing activities.

For the Love of
Women

MARIE ANDERSON

MV PUBLISHING

"Women bring us back into communication
with the eternal source, where God can
be seen clearly."

Ernest Renan

In my own mind, there is no coincidence between
the awakening of women and the fall of the Berlin
Wall, the end of the cold war and the development
of minority rights in our culture. The ascent of
women is a powerful engine for positive change
within society.

For the Love of Women is about the real power of
women. This power manifests itself in so many
ways that we can hardly understand the impact
upon our daily lives. In the mid-sixties, when
women realized that they were being excluded
from the mainstream of economic and political
development, they fought back. The fight occurred
on all levels of society – in the halls of government,
in the boardrooms and in the bedrooms. What we
began to grasp is that women are not just assets,
symbols or a commodity, they are rather a powerful force for growth and change. The women of
today, while conserving their essence of grace and
seduction, have taken on a more complex and
complete dimension within our lives. Ended are
the days when women would be content to stay
passively behind, while men went about running
things as they damn well pleased.

We hear increasingly that men don't really know how to be with women anymore. The traditional roles between men and women have changed and men are seeking a new identity. Well, there is no secret about it. Women are active and in communication. They are present in a real way for the first time - not living in hope but actually going out there and taking their rightful place. Men need to wake up and smell the coffee. If you want a relationship you had better acknowledge the presence of a complete and self-determined being and not some image in your mind about what a woman should or should not be.

And women also want to be women. They want to be beautiful and feminine, fall in love and be admired. Women want to get married and have kids. Women want to make men happy just as before, but not be effaced while doing it. Women want to be women but also demand respect and true loyalty from their men.

For the Love of Women is a series of dynamic snapshots of women. Women who love and want to be loved. Women who work hard and want the rewards that are coming to them. Women who cry for justice and ultimately prevail. Women who are soft and kind but also firm in their demand for self-determination and respect.

Marie Anderson

"The heart of a woman is like the sky above,
and like the sky, it changes night and day."

Lord Byron

"For the lamp to burn, we must add oil."

Mother Teresa

"Knowing men, I always assume
that women are right."

Georges Cabanis

"You may be disappointed if you fail
but you're lost if you don't try."

Beverly Sills

In Your Eyes

In your eyes
I see the daughter
I see the woman
I see the mother

In your eyes,
I see the end of all wars
I see the light of life burst forward
I see all the wide-open doors

In your eyes,
I see the future of all children
I see the joy of birth
I see the flight of the falcon

In your eyes,
I see the change in me
I see what I must become
I see the leaves, I see the branches, I see the tree

Marie Anderson

> "Woman is a ray of divine light."
>
> Djalal al-Din Rumi,
> Mathanawi

Women in History

- Joanne of Arc was born on January 6, 1412. On May 8, she liberated Orleans from the English;
- Rosine Bernard, known as Sarah Bernhardt was born in 1844. She greatly influenced the development of classical theatrical repertoire;
- Maria Sklodowska, better known as Marie Curie, doctor of physics, made many important discoveries in the area of radioactivity;
- Margaretha Geertruida Zelle, known as Mata Hari, was born in 1870 in Holland. Mata Hari played an important role as an intelligence agent during the First World War;
- Maria Montessori was born in 1870. She was the first woman medical doctor in Italy and she also developed a method of teaching known as the Montessori method;
- Gloria Steinem and Shulmith Firestone launched the Women's Lib movement in 1968 in the United States;
- In 1980, Margaret Thatcher became the first woman Prime Minister of England. She went on to be known as the Iron Lady.

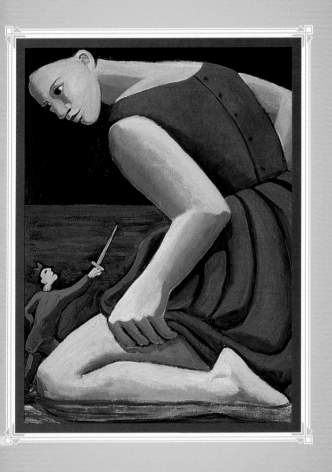

"Natural ability has been distributed in a similar fashion among the living and in the two sexes. Women must therefore take part in the same type of activities as men."

Plato

New Beginnings

I was forty-two when I went back to work. The kids were constantly telling me they were old enough to take care of themselves. I was feeling more and more useless as a mother. But when I told Bob, my husband, I wanted to go back to work he was dead set against it. He was sure the change would not be good. He had become used to having me around all the time. I realized I was not only his wife, I was his lover, his best friend, his confidante, his maid and his mother. Understandably, he felt he could only lose from my returning to work as he would no longer be the center of attention.

When, after a twenty-year hiatus, I returned to work, I saw that things had changed. I returned to the law office where I had worked as a secretary. Within a few months, they saw that I was quite able and asked whether I would be interested in training as a legal technician. That would allow me to learn more about the law and to help research and in the preparation of cases. I accepted without hesitation. This of course required that I study nights and weekends. I discovered that I really loved to study and that I had desired a real

challenge in my life. I was drinking it in. After less than a year, I completed my courses and was doing really interesting work for the firm. I enjoyed it so much and I was really good at it, so much so that I hinted at the possibility of going to law school to become a full-fledged lawyer, specializing in family law.

Meanwhile, back at home, Bob was becoming increasingly upset with me. Whenever we talked about my job and my desire to make a real career for myself, he found it hard to listen. I began to realize that as his career was starting to wind down, mine was just beginning. Bob was having a hard time giving up his notions of growing older as a couple, early retirement and home life in general. I was confronted with an important decision: move forward headlong in my career and risk losing my marriage or tone down the career plans and work at establishing a happy medium. I chose the latter.

I made arrangements to work three days a week at the firm, and Bob and I agreed that we would work till we were 60 and support each other fully until then. I didn't go for my law degree, but I saved something that was even more important to me – quality of life, family and love. I still have the stimulation of a challenging job, but I can still take time to smell the roses, take care of myself and spend a lot of quality time with my family.

Lucille T.

"Men always want to be the first love of
a woman. Women, on the other hand,
want to be the last love of a man."

Oscar Wilde

"A woman is the only gift that chooses you."

Anonymous

"By confronting our fears and becoming
conscious of the power within and beyond us
we can learn what courage is."

Anne Wilson-Schaef

"A woman who is a stranger to herself is also
a stranger to others."

Anne Morrow Lindberg

Sister of Mine

Oh, sister of mine
Where have you been
I have longed for you
I have waited for your return

Oh, daughter of mine
Must you leave me
Must you go
Must you take my heart with you when you go

Oh, mother of mine
I am so glad I found you
You are my ship, you are my heart
Take me with you where you go

Oh, wife of mine
Will you be there in my darkest hour
Will you hold my hand when I'm afraid
Will you travel with me where I must go

Marie Anderson

The Cycle of Death and Rebirth

I heard a very interesting idea the other day about reincarnation. Apparently, we've lived many lives before. We are forever caught in the cycle of death and of rebirth as the Buddhists believe. It is apparently a given that we have been both men and women in our past lives. This principle would account for many things. One of them is our innate ability to appreciate the other sex; we can appreciate the other because we have been the other sex in former lives.

Whether or not one believes in past lives, we are the artisans of the walls that divide us. Our ideas can create barriers and limitations. I believe that we can, with time, break down the barriers and live more freely and be more ourselves in all circumstances.

As women, we are confronted by outside forces of enormous magnitude. Although we have gained some level of freedom within our own culture, women around the world still struggle with enormous burdens. By living free and with self-respect, we light the way. By taking a firm stand on issues that affect all women, we light the way. By staying in communication and being willing to learn and to teach others, we light the way. By refusing to be objectified, abused, tormented and harassed, we light the way. By raising our children to be self-reliant, tolerant and open to change, we light the way.

Marie Anderson

Important Dates

- The first official tennis competition between women was held in Dublin, Ireland, in 1879;

- In 1905, Bertha Kinsky of Austria was the first woman to receive the Nobel Peace Prize;

- In 1910, at the age of 24, Élise Deroche was the first woman to earn a pilot's license;

- Lois Weber, in 1914, was the first woman to make a full-length feature film: *The Merchant of Venice*;

- The first Miss America was selected in 1921;

- Ellen Church, a nurse, became the first airline hostess, in 1930;

- In 1953, Ann Davidson was the first woman to cross the Atlantic in a sailboat;

- Junko Tabei was the first woman to reach the summit of Mount Everest, in 1975.

In the Real World

I went to an all-girl Catholic school when I was a child. We were taught by nuns. Although the nuns provided us with an excellent and rigorous education in mathematics, literature and the arts, their values and social perceptions were a little out of sync with the times. For them, women must be women in all circumstances. They must know their place and speak only when spoken to, using the right tone and manner.

However, the society around us was changing at a rapid rate and the nuns' teachings, while still of some value as a reference, were no longer completely adequate. For example, I was the one who had to pop the question to Tony. If I hadn't I don't think I would be married today. Tony is really shy. I think we went out for three months before I got my first kiss.

Another area where the sisters' training was a little out of step was in the treatment of children. Kids today need to communicate. They seem to grow up more rapidly than we did. They ask some of the wildest questions and they want answers. They want to be part of the family and be consulted on issues that concern them. The mother-child relationship is more complex today. Kids are young adults in their teens. They experience challenges and are confronted with realities we did not have to face until later on. Their school environment, the web, TV and their friends push them to grow

up so rapidly that they find it hard to cope sometimes. That's why we as parents have to be there as stable and loving figures in their lives. Most of the time, all this requires is the ability to listen, acknowledge and be there for them.

Another area that was completely ignored by the sisters is the art of love between men and women. I'm not just talking about sex, as this subject was completely taboo apart from the quick intro we received on the subject (to avoid getting pregnant out of wedlock). I'm talking about the basic ingredients that need to exist within a relationship for it to work, such as communication, respect, honesty and loyalty. Relationships with men were just never discussed. We were supposed to be good wives and mothers and this meant having a clean home and making good food. But life with a man is more demanding than that. It requires real patience and commitment to make a loving relationship work over time, especially because the world out there is a real jungle. I finished high school in the years of free love in the mid-seventies. Getting a man to listen and respect you was a real challenge. There was a lot of promiscuity in society and there still is. A woman has to fight to keep her man and to keep her self-respect. In this area, I'm a little more conservative. I believe that when you say, "I do," you do so for life, for better or worse and not until something better comes along. Fortunately, Tony and I have always stayed close and we haven't let outside influences wreck our marriage.

Betty-Lou D.

To Live a Long Life

Do you want to live to a ripe old age? The recipe is quite simple. A doctor who lived to the age of 107 has shared his recipe for longevity with us. He believed that if you place the head of your bed in a northerly direction, you will be aligning it with the great magnetic currents of Earth. If all I have to do to live to 107 years is to move my bed, I guess I'll try it.

To Live a Happy Life

An old doctor in writing to his son said this:

"Walk two hours a day. Sleep at least seven hours a day. Get up when you wake up. Start working from the moment you arise. Only eat when you are hungry and always eat slowly. Only drink when you are thirsty. Only talk when you have to and when you talk, only say half of the things you are thinking. Only write what you can sign. Do only the things that you can talk about. Don't forget that others will depend on you but that you must not depend on them. Don't overestimate the value of money. Money is a great servant but a very poor master."

Migraine Headaches

A cup of very strong black coffee with lemon juice mixed in can do wonders for a migraine headache.

Flight of Angels

An angel came to me last night
I laid there sleeping
And felt the touch so warm and so light
I opened mine eyes to see that loving face on wings

That sweet angel
Of love and light
Whispered her sweet gospel
And filled my heart with love and hope

She laid her gentle healing hand
Upon my heart so filled with tears
And took away the pain
I had once felt

She said that I was loved
And that she would watch over me
In this life and in the next
Until I found my way

Marie Anderson

"I believe that it is not the circumstances in which we find ourselves that determine our well-being, but rather the way we approach them."

Elizabeth King

"A woman must not depend on the protection of a man. She must learn to protect herself."

Susan Brownell Anthony

"Women find it easy to believe in the talents, abilities and fundamental goodness of others but they find it more difficult to believe in their own potential."

Sue Patton Theole

"Of course women want to be loved, but they also want to be entertained."

Bernard Le Bovier de Fontenelle

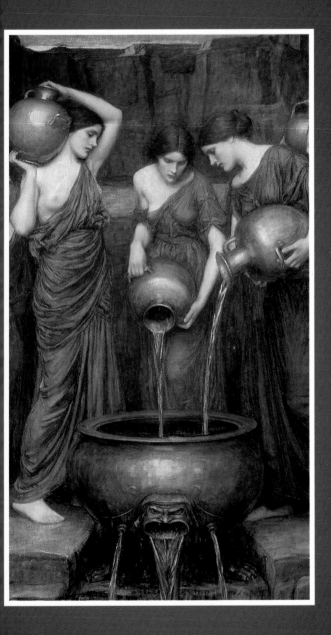

"The most complicated woman is closer
to nature than the simplest man."

Rémy de Gourmont

"Woman is God's masterpiece,
especially when she is mad."

Alphonse Allais

"Friendship for women is akin to love."

Thomas Moore

"Life is an adventure or not. Security does not
exist in nature and the children of men know
nothing of it. In the end, the easy way out is
no more certain then confronting real danger."

Helen Keller

In my own mind, there is no coincidence between the awakening of
and the fall of the Berlin Wall, the end of the Cold War; pe
Ireland; and the development of minority rights in our culture.
ascent of women is a powerful engine for positive change within s
For the Love of Women is about the real power of women. This
manifests itself in so many ways that we can hardly realize the
upon our daily lives. In the mid-sixties, when women realized the

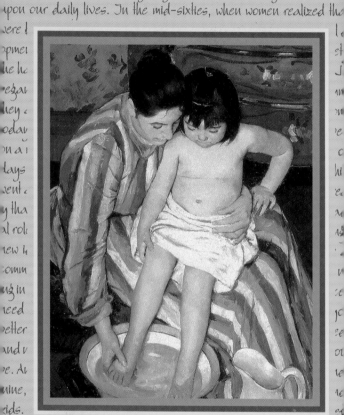

while doing it. Women want to be women but also demand respect an
oyalty from their men. For the Love of Women is a series of dy
snapshots of women. Women who love and want to be love. Wom
work hard and want the rewards that are coming to them. Women w
or justice and ultimately prevail. Women who are soft and kind bu
rm in their demand for self-determinism and respect.

The Power of One

I believe in the power of one
I keep my eye on the prize
I keep my eye on me
Until the job is done

The world I live in is rough
I put my trust in me
I put my best foot forward
I know I have to be tough

I kissed enough frogs to know
A girl has to save her kisses
A girl has to save her skin
That's the only way to go

I believe in the power of one
I believe in the power of my dreams
I believe in the power of abilities
I believe in me, because I'm the one

Marie Anderson

"Women are extreme. They are either better
or worse than men."

Jean de la Bruyère

People of the Shadows

In 1992, I was teaching at the university in anthropology as an associate professor. I decided to take a sabbatical, with the express idea of studying the Weyanna tribe on the northeastern tip of South America, something I had wanted to do for years. Based on our most recent studies, this was one of the last tribes that lived in a completely primitive state. They were known to be quite insular and did not welcome outsiders very often. Nevertheless, I was sure in my own mind that I could persuade them to let me live with them for the better part of a year. The result of this research would guarantee a permanent chair in the university.

I arrived in Georgetown, the capital of French Guyana, in mid-January, 1993. I was greeted by Marc Besson, a well-known anthropologist who had stayed with the Weyanna on and off over the previous five years and who had corresponded with me in my planning the trip. I had been expecting a short, bald professor type with thick glasses. Instead, I found a Robert Redford look-alike with a cute French accent who was absolutely charming. I was, in fact, quite taken aback, as I wasn't there thinking about my love life but rather about the scientific undertaking at hand. Nevertheless, I could sense a tingling feeling of delight when our

hands touched for the first time as he greeted me at the small Georgetown airport.

Reaching the Weyanna called for a four-day boat trip down the Tibotto River into the deep heart of the Guyanese rainforest. After a few days of preparation and time well spent getting to know each other, Marc and I set out with a small crew down the river. As we travelled through the lush rainforest, I found myself swept away by some current. I felt the pressures of modern life lifting away from me. I would catch myself laughing whenever Marc would make a slightly humorous statement. In fact, I felt a little like a schoolgirl out for a joy ride in the country, not at all the frame of mind you would expect to have as you approached a scientific endeavor that could alter your whole life. Nevertheless, I felt totally myself, totally at peace and I felt beautiful.

After three days of travel, Marc and I were sitting around the campfire having a drink before bedtime. It had been a long time since I had let my hair down. Marc and I were engaged in a conversation about why he had come to live here permanently when he had had everything back home in France – career, a beautiful home, prestige and admiration. "You know Anne, this meant absolutely nothing to me once I had attained it. I needed a new game. I was tired of the pretense of the intellectual bourgeoisie in France and the madness of life in Paris. We never talked about the real things

and I found I was stressed-out most of the time. When I came here, I blew a lot of emotional charge that I had pent up for years. I just never wanted to go back to it," said Marc.

I sat there lapping up every word as if I was drinking nectar from a flower. I was in love. I wanted this man and everything he stood for more than anything in the world. We kissed very passionately that night, but we didn't make love. I felt much too vulnerable and I wanted to make sure that this was the real thing.

Marc and I finally made it to the Weyanna. They knew him and welcomed him as a brother. And because I was with him they greeted me as a long-lost sister. We spent, during that first trip, ten weeks with "The People of the Shadows," as they called themselves. I learned so much. I learned about the simplest things. How to fish with a spear and cook a delicious meal the way the Weyanna do. How to make shelter in the forest. But mostly, I learned about myself, who I really am and what I really want from life. I learned how to be with another in a simple and uncomplicated way. I learned to hear and appreciate the natural music of life itself.

On May 19th, 1993, Marc and I were married. I now reside permanently in Georgetown in a very simple abode. We visit the Weyanna at least twice a year and do all that we can to protect them and to preserve their unblemished lifestyle. I can think of no better way to live my life.

Beatrice B.